# Leopard Gecko Facts for Kids

*Explore the Fascinating World of an Amazing Ground-Dwelling Lizard and Learn Everything You Need to Know About Them*

# Table of Contents

Introduction ..................................................................1

Chapter 1: Introduction ............................................... 3

Chapter 2: Meet the Leopard Gecko ............................. 11

Chapter 3: Setting Up the Perfect
Leopard Gecko Home .................................................. 21

Chapter 4: Feeding and Nutrition ............................... 29

Chapter 5: Health and Wellness ................................... 37

Chapter 6: Fun Facts and Quirky Behavior .................. 49

Chapter 7: Engaging Activities for Children ................. 56

Chapter 8: Frequently Asked Questions ....................... 64

Conclusion ................................................................ 71

References ................................................................. 73

# Introduction

Leopard geckos are fascinating ground-dwelling creatures with unique characteristics and delightful habits. But why are they called leopard geckos? Are they as fierce as a leopard? What does "gecko" mean in the first place? This book will answer all these questions and more!

The first chapter starts with a brief overview of these creatures and why they make excellent pets for children. You will learn the importance of caring for them properly rather than letting them be.

The next chapter will dive into their appealing characteristics. Why are they so different from other lizards? What sizes do they come in, and how long do they live?

You will be introduced to their natural habitat in the wild. How do they survive in the wild if they need proper care? The common varieties of leopard geckos will also be discussed.

You will go on to understand how to build their ideal home in your house and recreate their natural environment step by step. What is their pet house called? How big should it be? Do you need to keep it at a specific temperature? Which accessories and playthings can you decorate it with?

Then, you will learn how to feed your favorite pet. What do they eat, and how much? How often should you feed them? This chapter will provide a detailed feeding schedule.

You will then understand how to keep them healthy and what to do if they look unhealthy. The next chapter will discuss an extensive list of fun facts about them and their interesting behaviors, along with a wide range of exciting activities for children.

This book is an easy read for both children and adults. You will learn everything about caring for leopard geckos from scratch, making it ideal for first-timers, and experienced pet owners will discover many singular facts and techniques throughout.

# Chapter 1: Introduction

Leopard geckos aren't as huge and fierce as leopards, so don't think you will own a fearsome beast. "Gecko" is a type of lizard, a creature whose length is greater than its breadth or width. It has a long, thick tail, four flexible limbs, two tiny eyes, and a skin consisting of scales. Unlike other types of lizards, geckos prefer the night to the day, making them nocturnal lizards. Like leopards, they have black spots on their skin, which is why they are called leopard geckos. These spots are usually present on a yellow and white skin, but their colors and textures can be numerous.

1.   *The leopard gecko. Source: https://www.pexels.com/photo/close-up-shot-of-leopard-gecko-on-white-textile-5475195/*

# Brief Overview of Leopard Geckos

As soon as you lay eyes on a leopard gecko, you will immediately know it is a lizard. It has a tapered head like a miniature dragon, dark eyes that look like just another spot on the skin, a long body with a bulge in the middle for a stomach, and a lengthy tail like a snake's. Its most distinguishing feature is the black spots on its body, which come in many shapes and sizes.

In the wild, leopard geckos are found in arid (dry) desert areas or rocky regions. If you want to see them in their wild habitat, head to the dry grasslands and deserts of India, Nepal, Pakistan, Iran, and Afghanistan. They are scientifically called Eublepharis macularius, a Greek name that loosely means "good eyelid spots." It is a direct reference to the spots on its body and the presence of eyelids that are unique to this species.

Zoologists have found five subspecies of leopard geckos so far, each based on its country of origin (India, Nepal, Pakistan, Iran, or Afghanistan). In the United States, you won't usually find a wild lizard native to these countries. Most of the leopard geckos here are captive species, bred in a controlled habitat so they can safely flourish away from the dangers of their wild terrain.

Since they are nocturnal animals, how do they survive in the scorching heat of the desert, you may wonder. They hide beneath rocks or within crevices, and when they can find a tree, they reside under its loose bark. When day turns to night, they come out of their hideouts to perch atop rocks to get warm. You see, the sun may have set, but the rocks can stay hot for hours.

*2.  In the wild, they are found in dry desert or rocky areas. Source: https://www.rawpixel.com/image/5935620/free-public-domain-cc0-photo*

Leopard geckos prefer meat but don't mind eating vegetables. In the wild, they eat many tiny invertebrates (creatures without a backbone), like crickets and locusts. Ideally, you should feed them a healthy mix of meat and veggies.

---

## Why Leopard Geckos Make Great Pets for Children

The popularity of leopard geckos is rapidly rising. Did you know they are second only to the bearded dragon in the lizard community? Children like to keep lizards as pet, and they usually go for leopard geckos. Indeed, if you love lizards, a leopard gecko has to be one of your creatures of choice.

However, why are they excellent pets for children like you? Why not a dog or a cat? Aren't lizards slimy, slippery little things?

---

- **They Aren't Slimy:** Unlike many other reptiles you may know, leopard geckos aren't slimy or dirty at all. Since they prefer a dry environment, their bodies are quite dry. They shed their skin often, which makes them cleaner than most other pets. They (and you) will have a lot of fun perched on your shoulder, blinking their little eyes at you like a clueless toddler.

- **Their Size:** Dogs and cats are a handful, especially for children with little hands. Leopard geckos are small and can easily fit into the palm of their hand. Are you thinking of getting your first pet? A leopard gecko will be more fun, especially since you can hold it in your hand.

- **Their Maintenance:** They don't need constant attention, unlike some other pets. You can build their home easily, and once they are inside, you can just leave them be. Since they shed their skin, you don't need to bathe them. Just feed them and watch these adorable creatures crawl around in their space.

- **Their Nature:** Leopard geckos are known for their calm and gentle temperament, making them less likely to bite or become aggressive. If your first interaction with them goes smoothly and they become friendly, they will almost never bite you. If they do (on very rare occasions), don't fret because their bite won't hurt or harm you in any way.

- **Their Ability to be Handled:** Children can easily handle and care for geckos, as they are not as skittish as many other reptiles. However, you should take care you don't hurt them. Improper handling may lead to their death. Learn the proper handling techniques before buying one as a pet.

- **Their Educational Value:** Keeping a leopard gecko allows you to learn about biology, ecology, and responsible pet care. You can observe its behavior, learn about its habitat, understand its dietary needs, and so much more. If you want educational entertainment, learn interesting facts about these creatures.

- **Their Lifespan:** They can live for 10 to 20 years or more with proper care. Since childhood lasts for 12-15 years, your pet leopard will be your companion throughout your growing years.

- **Their Variety:** While the most common leopard geckos look like leopards (yellow and white colors with black spots), they come in many colors and patterns, from bright orange to black.

- **Their Demeanor:** Compared to most other pets, they are quiet. They scream or squeal only when there's a predator around, and they rarely produce a sound in a controlled environment like your home.

## The Importance of Understanding and Caring for Leopard Geckos

If leopard geckos can thrive perfectly well in the wild, why should you adopt them as pets? They are low-maintenance, so why should you care for them after adoption? Why is it necessary to understand these spotted reptiles of the arid regions?

*3. Having a leopard gecko as a pet will teach you many valuable life lessons! Source: https://www.pexels.com/photo/close-up-shot-of-a-person-holding-a-leopard-gecko-8162455/*

- **Teaches Responsibility:** Caring for any living creature, not just the leopard gecko, teaches responsibility, which is an important life skill for everyone. Caring for a leopard gecko implies feeding it and cleaning and maintaining its habitat. You will understand exactly what it means to be responsible for someone.

- **Increases Their Lifespan:** Wild leopard geckos usually don't live full lives due to the presence of predators and harsh conditions. However, their lifespan may be increased as a pet.

- **Animal Welfare Awareness:** Leopard geckos, like all animals, deserve to be treated with respect. They need proper care to ensure their health and well-being, without which they may die and eventually become extinct. Understanding their needs helps prevent neglect or mistreatment.

- **Provides Educational Value:** Caring for them can be an educational experience, teaching you about nature, wildlife, and animal behavior. You get to learn about the environment and the importance of its conservation.

- **Teaches Empathy:** Empathy and compassion are important when caring for a living creature. You will understand their needs and feelings, which will help you behave properly with your fellow human beings.

- **Bonding:** Building a bond with a leopard gecko is a rewarding experience. They prefer solitude but don't mind being held from time to time. When your friends and family aren't around, they will be your companions, comforting you.

- **Mental Health Benefits:** No matter how bad your day has been, you will feel completely relaxed playing with your leopard gecko. Simply holding your favorite pet will lower your stress levels and make you feel refreshed to do your homework or finish your daily chores.

- **Understanding Ecology:** Did you know leopard geckos play an important role in maintaining ecological balance? They aren't like those lazy sloths or meddlesome rats. In the wild, a variety of insects form a main part of their diet. They help control the population and bring balance to the environment. Indeed, without geckos, the world's insect population may have spiraled out of control.

Leopard geckos make exciting pets and benefit the environment. Is your house buzzing with insects? Your pet gecko might just help you reduce their numbers!

# Chapter 2: Meet the Leopard Gecko

Mere pictures of leopard geckos don't do justice to these fascinating creatures. They cannot provide a well-rounded view of the gecko. Several subtle aspects of its physical makeup aren't easily visible unless you specifically look for them. Before meeting your leopard gecko for the first time, you should know its background, characteristics, habitat, and the different varieties.

## Physical Characteristics

*4.   They look like a mix between a lizard and a mini dragon! Source: https://commons.wikimedia.org/wiki/File:Juvenile-leopard-gecko.jpg*

Leopard geckos look like most small lizards—miniature versions of mythical dragons and long-extinct dinosaurs. They are long and thin, with four limbs and a neck indistinguishable from the rest of their body. They have flat feet, but unlike other species of geckos, they don't stick, meaning the creature struggles to climb flat, vertical surfaces like smooth walls. Instead, they have claws to climb rough inclines.

Two main characteristics distinguish leopard geckos from other geckos. First, they have movable eyelids that can be shut while sleeping, although they aren't as distinctive as human eyelids. The eyes of other geckos are lidless or immovable. Second (you may have already guessed this), they have dark spots on their body, specifically on their dorsal (back) and ventral (front) sides.

Did you know full-grown leopard geckos have 100 teeth? Humans can regrow their teeth only twice in their lifetime, but your pet lizard's teeth are replaced every three to four months (unlimited times!). Their tail is normally thick and long, but they can store fat for a rainy day. Their tail becomes even thicker and bulky when fat is stored.

## Unique Patterns and Colors

Wild leopard geckos are normally yellow-white or brown-white. Their dorsal side is yellow or brown, and the ventral side is white. Their spots are either dark brown or black. However, the captive-bred species come in many more attractive patterns and colors.

- **Hypo:** Hypomelanistic leopard geckos have reduced melanin pigment (a substance in the body responsible for skin color), resulting in a lighter overall appearance. They often have brighter and more vivid colors with light shades.

*5.   Hypomelanistic leopard gecko. Source: https://www.needpix.com/photo/download/340007/leopard-gecko-gecko-yellow-hump-reptile-leopard-lizard-animal-nature*

- **Albino:** Albino leopard geckos cannot produce melanin. They have virtually no dark spots. They ideally have white or yellow bodies with pink or red eyes.

*6.   Albino leopard gecko. Source: https://www.flickr.com/photos/b_heyer/8809792901*

**Morphs:** Numerous morphs have been selectively bred to exhibit specific patterns and colors. A few popular morphs among children are:

- **Tangerine:** Tangerine leopard geckos have vibrant orange or tangerine-colored bodies.

7.  *Tangerine leopard gecko. Source:*
*https://www.flickr.com/photos/143146286@N02/52319111864*

- **High Yellow:** They have a lot of yellow coloration with minimal dark markings.

- **Patternless:** They lack the distinct spots seen in wild geckos, which gives them a more uniform appearance.

- **Blizzard:** They have a white or pale gray body with little to no pattern.

*8.  Blizzard leopard gecko. Source:*
*https://www.flickr.com/photos/leguan001/3365521831*

- **Jungle:** They have a more banded or striped pattern along their bodies.

- **Mack Snow:** They are heavily melanized, with dark bands or stripes on a lighter background color.

- **Emerine:** They have a unique pattern characterized by dark spots outlined in white or light coloration, giving them a distinct appearance.

- **Enigma:** Enigma leopard geckos have a pattern characterized by irregular, chaotic blotches and spots. From afar, they look like opaque marbles.

- **Raptor:** This is a combination of albino and patternless variants. A unique breed among geckos, it usually has orange-white bodies with dark red eyes.

## Size and Lifespan

Leopard geckos are so small that you can hold one in your palms. When they are born, they are around three to four inches long. However, they don't grow much beyond that. Adults reach a maximum size of 10 inches, but most captive geckos are around eight inches long. Females are generally shorter, while males grow longer.

*9. Adults reach a maximum size of 10 inches. Source: https://www.flickr.com/photos/132295270@N07/33544745134*

They grow no larger than 1 and a half inches in width and weigh around two ounces. If they somehow lose their tail (it gets cut on a rock, or they drop it themselves!), their weight decreases, but they can regrow the tail and regain the lost weight.

They may have many defense mechanisms (discussed in the next section), but wild leopard geckos tend to die off within 10 years. However, that's not their maximum lifespan. They fall prey to creatures like foxes and other large reptiles, or the temperature and environmental extremes kill them off. But in captivity where there are no predators and the environmental conditions can be controlled, they have the potential to double their lifespan, with some creatures reaching 20 years or more.

## Habitat in the Wild

Leopard geckos don't roam the forests, grasslands, or deserts in the U.S. They are native to the arid regions of south-central Asia, primarily in Afghanistan, Pakistan, northwest India, and parts of Iran. Rocky deserts and semi-desert areas are their preferred habitat, but they can also thrive in dry grasslands and forests.

They have developed an adaptation unique to arid regions with low humidity. They can live a healthy life in areas with sparse vegetation, rocky outcrops, and sand. Like bats and owls, they are nocturnal creatures. They spend their days hiding in rocky crevices, burrows, or other natural shelters to avoid the intense daytime heat. These shelters also act as protection from predators and extreme environmental conditions.

However, leopard geckos are cold-blooded, meaning their bodies cannot generate heat. They need to take it from their surroundings. Since they prefer to hide from the sun, how do they get the required heat to maintain their body temperature? The thing is, even after the sun has set, Mother Earth can retain her heat for several hours. When the leopard geckos crawl out of their shelters at night, they absorb heat from the ground and surrounding rocks.

Apart from absorbing heat, leopard geckos also hunt at night. They can eat anything edible if they can hunt or forage for it, but they prefer to feed on insects, spiders, and other small invertebrates. They generally smell out their prey before seeing and catching it. Food may be easily available in their habitat, but water sources can be scarce in an arid climate. They obtain most of their water from their prey and have adapted to survive without direct water sources.

## Common Varieties of Leopard Geckos

Apart from the variants discussed in a previous section based on their colors and patterns, leopard geckos come in many more varieties.

- **Eclipse:** They are a morph of a common, yellow-colored leopard gecko with eyes as black as night. Their bright yellow eyelids act as the circumference of the sun, making you feel as if you're staring into an eclipse. They are bred in many other colors and patterns.

*10. Eclipse leopard gecko. Source:*
*https://www.pexels.com/photo/close-up-shot-of-leopard-gecko-on-white-textile-5475191/*

- **Carrot Tail:** As the name suggests, they have a tail that resembles a carrot. The rest of their body and spot markings can be of any color or pattern, but their tail is a bright orange with patches of white.

*11. Carrot tail. Source:*
*https://www.needpix.com/photo/download/1690762/gecko-leopard-gecko-climb-wall-reptile-free-pictures-free-photos-free-images-royalty-free*

- **Super Giants:** Don't let the name mislead you. They are a slightly larger variety of leopard geckos that can reach 12 inches in length and weigh around four ounces.

- **Tremper:** Unlike the other varieties whose names define some features of the gecko, Tremper is named after its creator, a renowned breeder called Ron Tremper. It looks like an albino leopard gecko from afar, but its body has various complex patterns that separate it from the rest.

*12. Tremper albino. Source:*
*https://www.needpix.com/photo/download/1298358/reptiles-*
*nature-animals-free-pictures-free-photos-free-images-royalty-free-*
*free-illustrations*

- **Aberrant:** The spots on most other leopard geckos are evenly distributed. On the aberrant variant, the spots are generally larger, and distinct gaps between them make the creature unique to its species.

# Chapter 3: Setting Up the Perfect Leopard Gecko Home

Tanner always wanted a leopard gecko. It wasn't until his 10th birthday that his parents decided to get him one. The little boy lit up like a Christmas tree when he got his new pet. He couldn't contain his joy. He named his new friend Winnie. Tanner was so happy that he gets to finally share his room with his favorite pet. He wanted his gecko to truly feel at home so he decided to create a home as wonderful as his bedroom for his new friend, somewhere the leopard gecko could also play and feel safe. With this mission in mind, Tanner set out to give his pet the perfect bedroom in a tank with the help of his parents.

*13. Creating the ideal terrarium should be at the top of your list.
Source:
https://upload.wikimedia.org/wikipedia/commons/a/a8/Bioactive
_Arid_Vivarium.jpg*

In this chapter, you'll learn how to transform a simple tank into a miniature paradise, as Tanner did for his pet, creating a 'home' where your gecko can feel safe and snug. Now, you might be wondering why this chapter is so important. Just as how you need a cozy bed and your favorite toys, leopard geckos need a comfy, safe space to thrive and play. It's time for you to discover how to make the perfect home for a leopard gecko. Are you ready to make it happen? Grab your toolbox.

## Creating the Ideal Terrarium

The word "terrarium" is just a fancy way of saying a small, pretty garden inside a see-through box. Terrariums can have plants or small animals, which people keep for a few reasons. Some people like them because they look like a nice decoration in their house. Others use them to study animals or plants up close, and some even use them to breed animals. Think of the terrarium as their very own kingdom, where they rule with tiny lizard crowns. To get started, take note of the following:

- The terrarium box should be see-through. Glass terrariums are popular because you can easily peek in on your gecko, and they're easy to clean. Plastic terrariums work, too, but glass holds heat a little better, and your gecko needs all the heat it can get to stay warm.

- There should be a door for easy access. Look for a terrarium that opens from the front like a mini fridge. This way, you can easily clean the tank and care for your leopard gecko.

- The lid must be very secure to stop your curious gecko from turning into a Houdini and exploring on its own. A lid also keeps the temperature and humidity just right inside their home.

## Size and Space Requirements

Can you do cartwheels in a phone booth? No, right? Well, your leopard gecko doesn't like to be stuffed in small boxes, either. They need space to stretch out, climb, and move around. So, when setting up their home, make sure it's big enough for them to do whatever they want without restrictions.

Give your gecko a tank that's 24 inches long, 16 inches high, and 12 inches deep. This tank size gives your gecko enough room to move around comfortably and allows for good air circulation to keep them healthy.

## Substrate Choices

The substrate refers to the ground beneath your leopard gecko's feet. It is like the carpet in their mini palace. The floor is important because your leopard gecko will hang out on it all the time. There are lots of different choices for gecko floors, but not all of them are safe. Here are some of the best options that won't make your gecko ill:

- **You can get paper towels.** They are cheap, easy to clean, and great for baby geckos.

- **Rock slates are also a good option.** They are flat, smooth, easy to clean, and will certainly look nice in the terrarium.

- **Special reptile carpets are also available.** These carpets are specially made for reptile cages. Get one that is easy to clean and doesn't have loose threads that your gecko could eat. Things like that can make them fall sick.

## Temperature and Lighting Needs

Just like how you like your room to be nice and warm, your gecko friend needs the right temperature and lighting. This helps to make them more comfortable and relaxed in their new home.

*14. You have to make sure that the temperature and lighting are perfect so your leopard gecko is happy and comfortable. Source: https://pxhere.com/en/photo/1194535#google_vignette*

**Lighting Basics**

1. **Daylight Hours:** Try to mimic the seasons. Give your gecko 14 hours of daylight and 10 hours of darkness during summer, and then 12 hours of daylight of 12 hours of nightlight during winter season.

2. **Natural Light Is Enough:** You won't need to provide an extra source of lightning if your gecko's tank gets enough natural sunlight during the day.

3. **No Night Light:** Bright lights at night mess up your gecko's sleep. Stick to low light if you need to see them at night.

4. **Vitamin D Power:** UVB light helps leopard geckos get Vitamin D3, which is important for their health. If no UVB light is available, you can use supplements. Talk to an adult or a professional to help you with that.

## Lighting Options

1. **Standard Lighting:** Soft white incandescent bulbs or halogen flood lamps are good choices.

2. **UVB Light:** Look for T8 or T5 UVB reptile lights specifically designed for reptiles.

## What Are Their Temperature Needs?

**They Need a Spot for Basking:** Leopard geckos need their warm spots. As the cold-blooded animals that they are, a warm spot should not be lacking in their tanks. This is the area where your gecko goes to heat up. The temperature here should be 90-95 degrees Fahrenheit (32-35 degrees Celsius). There are special lamps used to create these basking spots, they are called heat lamps.

**They Also Need a Cool Side:** The temperature in this spot should be around 75-80 degrees Fahrenheit (24-27 degrees Celsius) so your gecko can chill and relax. The ambient temperature in the room usually achieves the cooler side, but depending on your climate, you might need additional heating or cooling.

# Essential Accessories and Hideouts

Last but not least, time to add some flair to your gecko's palace with essential accessories and hideouts. These hideouts give your gecko friend a sense of security and privacy.

## Hideouts

Your gecko needs a warm hideout and a cool hideout. This allows them to choose the perfect spot to relax, depending on their mood. Cork bark rounds, flat rocks, or small reptile hides from pet stores are all great options. Make sure the hides are big enough for your gecko to fit in comfortably but not too big where they will feel exposed.

## Essentials

- **Water is important.** A shallow dish with fresh, clean water is a must-have. Change it daily to keep it sparkling clean.

- **Get a food dish for them.** Choose a shallow, easy-to-clean one if you're using a separate feeding dish.

- **Provide climbing rocks and branches**. Give your gecko some exercise opportunities with smooth rocks and branches to climb on.

- **Add some plant-tastic vibes.** Live plants add decoration, help with humidity, and can be fun for your gecko to explore. Choose plants that are safe and easy to care for.

You have been equipped with all you need to build a fantastic home for your leopard gecko. So go on and set up the perfect home. As you do so, remember that leopard geckos should be treated individually because they all have different preferences. Pay attention to their behavior so you can make adjustments where and when necessary to create and maintain an environment where your leopard gecko can feel safe and secure.

# Chapter 4: Feeding and Nutrition

While some reptiles are carnivores and some herbivores, leopard geckos only feed on live and moving insects in their natural habitat. Besides feeding them live insects, leopard geckos can also be fed commercially available feed consisting of dried insects. Keep reading as this chapter has all the necessary information you may need while taking care of and feeding your adorable reptilian pet.

*15. Leopard geckos get the best nutrition from dry or live insects.*
*Source: https://www.stockvault.net/photo/236154/little-gecko*

# Understanding Leopard Gecko Diets

Leopard geckos are insectivores and must only be given a diet consisting exclusively of live insects. They thrive on a protein-rich diet and don't have a digestive system that can digest plant matter. The insects you can feed them include crickets, phoenix worms (calci worms), locusts, mealworms, silkworms, dubia roaches, and waxworms. Just like you must feed them healthy and pest-free insects, it's also crucial to keep the size of the insects in check. The insects you feed cannot be larger than the distance between your flashy reptile's eyes.

# Choosing the Right Food

### Variety for Balanced Nutrition

Offering different insect species will give your gecko variety and well-balanced nutrition. Each type of insect has different nutrients, and by rotating them, you can prevent nutritional imbalances that may arise from feeding a single type of insect exclusively.

### Gut-Loading

This maintains your gecko's health. In gut-loading, you will feed nutritious foods to the insects before offering them to the gecko. The insect's nutritional content will increase, ensuring that the gecko receives plenty of vitamins and minerals. You can gut-load the insects with any vegetable or fruit. However, never gut-load the insects with broccoli, spinach, and acidic vegetables or fruits. Furthermore, remember that the insects must be gut-loaded twelve hours before your gecko's feeding time. Loading the insects early allows them to break down the nutrients, making it easier for your gecko to assimilate the required nutrients.

## Calcium Supplements

Your Leopard gecko needs a constant supply of calcium to keep their bones strong. The best way to dust the insects is with a calcium supplement (without vitamin D3). It must be done at least two to three times a week. Likewise, a weekly or monthly multivitamin supplement can also be given using dusting. To dust the insects, take a plastic bag, add insects, and dust them lightly with the powder. It is best to dust insects before feeding time. If the insects are challenging to handle, lowering the surrounding temperature can slow their movements.

## Feeding Frequency

While adult geckos can go without food for days (two to three days), young leopard geckos must be fed daily. It's necessary to adjust your pet's feeding frequency according to their age, size, and activity level to maintain a healthy weight and prevent obesity. The best way to know how many insects to feed is to measure their body length and add two insects for every inch.

## Hydration

While leopard geckos obtain moisture from the insects they consume, you must still keep a shallow dish of clean, fresh water inside the enclosure. Some geckos may not drink directly from a dish; in that case, maintain hydration by occasionally misting the enclosure or placing water droplets on the gecko's nose.

## Temperature and Digestion

The body temperature of leopard geckos is significantly influenced by the external environment. You must maintain two different temperatures in the enclosure with the basking spot around 88-90°F (31-32°C), while the cooler side around 75-80°F (24-27°C).

## Avoid Wild-Caught Insects

You must only feed your pet commercially bred live insects or commercially available dried insect feed. Refrain from feeding a bug or a familiar live insect from your garden or backyard, as these wild insects can carry harmful pesticides. Avoid feeding your gecko wild-caught insects, as they may carry parasites or have been exposed to pesticides. Stick to commercially bred insects to be safe.

## Monitoring for Allergies

Pay attention to your gecko's preferences and any signs of allergies or aversions to certain insects. If you notice your gecko doesn't like certain insects, tell your veterinarian. Common signs include reduced activity and food regurgitation. If there is an undetected illness, your gecko may shed skin abnormally, have problems with egg laying, or even lose its tail.

## Feeding Schedule

Leopard geckos grow rapidly for up to 6 months and need food daily to support their development.

Adult leopard geckos up to one year should be fed daily with one day a week of skipped meals.

Leopard geckos older than a year can be fed every other two days or even three days.

Please keep in mind that you may need to tweak your gecko's diet according to their metabolism and health. A quick check in with the vet can help you out in making a tailored feeding schedule.

Follow the instructions for feeding frequency if you are using commercial food. However, when feeding them live insects, don't forget to apply the feeding rule where you feed two insects for every inch of the gecko's body length.

**Portion Control**

**Size of Prey Items:** Offer appropriately sized prey items. As mentioned earlier, the general guideline is to avoid insects larger than the space between the gecko's eyes to prevent choking and ensure smooth digestion.

**Quantity:** You can also divide the insects into smaller portions, making it easier for your gecko to consume within 15-20 minutes. When you portion feed your pet, there won't be uneaten prey left behind, eliminating any chances of microbial development.

**Monitoring Weight:** Keeping a tab on your leopard gecko weight is crucial. If there is a prominent shift in weight, contact a certified veterinarian to prevent issues like obesity or malnutrition and an effective action plan.

**Feeding During Hibernation**

Just like mammals hibernate, leopard geckos undergo brumation. During this time, your leopard gecko will show reduced activity due to a decrease in metabolism and feeding urge. It can occur in a few geckos aged over a year. Although they don't need to go through brumation, some reptiles may naturally want to brumate. In this situation, you will see reduced appetite, more time spent in the enclosure's cooler area, and more sleep.

When you suspect your gecko is going into brumation, keep the temperature gradient within the enclosure stable to help them regulate their body temperature. Over time, you will notice them becoming dormant and not showing an eagerness to feed. During this time, reduce their feeding frequency, offer small portions, and keep an eye on your adorable reptile for signs of distress, weight loss, or a disease.

For first-timers, consulting once with the vet about their brumation period can set you up to deal with the relevant challenges without a hitch.

## Tips for Feeding Right

- Always follow a feeding schedule whether you have a baby gecko or an adult. Making a schedule ensures that your gecko is always fed, especially when you have to feed an adult gecko every two or three days.

- Keep a feeding journal where you must note down the type of insects and the insect count. The logs help you prevent obesity or malnutrition.

*16. Keep a journal to keep track of how and when you feed your new friend! Source: https://www.rawpixel.com/image/6860681/png-sticker-book*

- It is necessary to have a designated feeding enclosure as it prevents your gecko from gulping down the sand and gravel with their food.

- No matter how quickly your gecko finishes its meal, stick to the feeding schedule and avoid overfeeding them.

- Keep a tab on how well your gecko is eating. If there's a red flag, contact the vet for the necessary intervention.

- If your leopard gecko has a habit of feeding on a specific insect, they may reject eating a new species of insect. Vets recommend raising your gecko on a mix of live insects they can consume safely. However, for picky eaters, give your gecko time to recognize and adjust to its new prey. In situations like these, you can also use a feeding tong to stimulate your gecko's predatory instincts to hunt and eat.

- Although feeding geckos live insects is preferable, baby geckos are mostly fed pre-killed insects. When your juvenile gecko is transitioning to an adult, start introducing live insects as keeping them on pre-killed insects can make them hesitant to feed on live insects.

- For egg-laying females, it's best to consult the vet for the necessary calcium and mineral supplementation.

# Chapter 5: Health and Wellness

Just like any species from the animal kingdom, leopard geckos can develop health anomalies, diseases, and conditions. As a leopard gecko owner, it's necessary to put in effort and educate yourself about the common health issues your gecko may develop. Here are the main ones you should know:

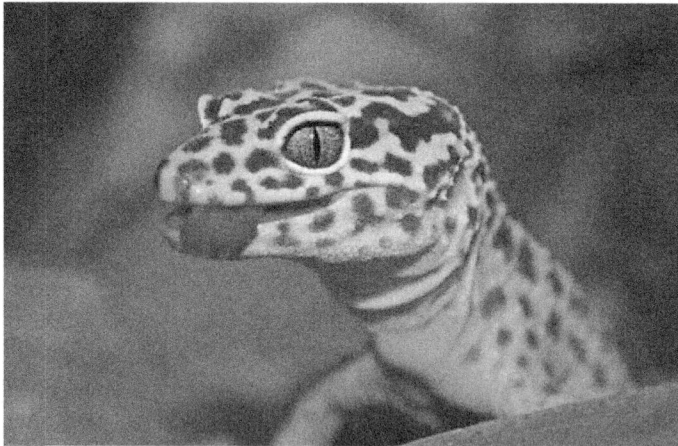

*17.  You need to know how to spot any strange behavior so you can treat the risk of disease from early on. Source: https://www.flickr.com/photos/eternalphotography/3369860368*

# Metabolic Bone Disease (MBD)

This is a condition that affects bone health and is difficult to diagnose. Although it's deadly, you can treat it by feeding calcium, Vitamin D3, and nutritious gut-loaded insects.

**Signs:** Shaking, mobility issues, crooked spine, leg deformities, constipation, loss of appetite.

## Causes

- Giving inadequate calcium in the diet can lead to a deficiency, worsening bone health.

- Lack of proper UVB lighting can be an aggravating factor, as the light is essential for your gecko's calcium metabolism and vitamin D synthesis.

- Feeding your gecko an improper calcium-to-phosphorus ratio can stop proper nutrient absorption, causing MBD.

# Impaction

This happens when your gecko's digestive tract becomes blocked.

**Signs:** Constipation, decreased or absence of fecal output, lethargy, bloating, straining during defecation.

## Causes

- When your gecko accidently eats substrate like sand or gravel.

- Foods that may be difficult to ingest or too large.

- Temperature shits in the enclosure or dehydration.

# Respiratory Infections

**Signs:** Labored breathing, wheezing, open-mouth breathing, nasal discharge, lethargy, decrease in appetite.

## Causes

- Inadequate temperature and humidity levels can cause microbial growth, leading to breathing problems.

- Poor ventilation in the enclosure stops airflow, increasing the risk of infections.

- A poor immune system or distress can also increase the risk of respiratory infections.

# Parasitic Infections

**Signs:** Weight loss, decrease in appetite, diarrhea, visible parasites in feces or around the vent, lethargy, weakness.

## Causes

- There's an increased risk of getting internal parasites if you are feeding your gecko contaminated food or water.

- They have high chances of catching a parasitic infection when exposed to animals already infected with parasites.

- Likewise, a stressed gecko or one with a weak immune system is more vulnerable to parasites.

# Dystocia (Egg-Binding)

**Signs:** Lethargy, loss of appetite, visible swelling of the abdomen, discomfort in the abdominal area, straining, or inability to lay eggs.

*18. Dystocia makes it difficult for the leopard gecko to lay eggs. Source: https://www.flickr.com/photos/thelizardwizard/3012662256*

## Causes

- Insufficient calcium levels affect eggshell formation and lead to difficulties in laying eggs.

- Improper nesting conditions like adding inadequate substrate for egg-laying in the enclosure.

Although egg-binding happens when calcium levels drop, defective genes can cause complications during the egg-laying process.

# Tail Loss

**Signs:** Sudden shedding of the tail, visible wound or bleeding at the tail base, regrowth of a smaller tail.

## Causes

- Handling stress may trigger a defensive response, leading to tail shedding.

- Predatory threat or aggression from cage mates can also result in tail loss.

# Eye Infections

**Signs:** Swelling or redness around the eyes, discharge from the eyes, squinting or keeping eyes closed, rubbing, or pawing at the eyes.

## Causes

- Poor cleanliness in the enclosure.

- Inflammation and abrasions can occur if substrate particles stick to their eyes.

- Poor hygiene of your gecko can give way to bacterial or fungal infections.

# Mouth Rot (Stomatitis)

**Signs:** Redness or swelling around the mouth, drooling, difficulty eating, foul odor from the mouth, visible lesions or ulcers.

## Causes

- Unclean water and feeding dishes are one of the causes of mouth infections.

- Abrasions or injuries to the mouth, possibly from rough surfaces or aggressive cage mates.

- Bacterial or fungal infections that affect the oral cavity.

---

# Obesity

**Signs:** Excessive weight gain, obvious overweight appearance, decreased activity levels, difficulty moving.

*19. Obesity happens to geckos, too, and it's important not to overfeed them. Source:*
*https://www.flickr.com/photos/silkebaron/31091704592*

## Causes

- Giving your gecko insects with a high-calorie content or overfeeding them.

- Limited space in the enclosure, lack of hiding spots, and decreased physical activity can also result in weight problems.

---

# Neurological Issues

**Signs:** Difficulty coordinating movements, tremors, paralysis, abnormal behaviors (circling, head tilting), seizures.

## Causes

- Vitamin deficiencies, particularly a lack of vitamin B.

- Infectious diseases affecting the nervous system can lead to neurological issues.

---

# Thermal Burns

Leopard geckos get thermal burns, injuring their skin when they come into contact with the heat source surfaces that regulate temperature.

**Signs:** Redness, blistering, swelling, skin damage. The uppermost skin layer can die (necrotize), exposing the skin's tissue.

## Causes

- If your gecko comes in contact with a heated surface like rocks, lids covering heat lamps, or under-tank heaters.

In case of a thermal burn, care by a certified vet is mandatory. They have the exact knowledge to treat the burn and prevent further infection.

# Preventive Measures

Although your first step should be to consult a vet, the general measures shared here can protect your adorable reptile pet from various problems related to health.

- Keep the enclosure humidity and temperature levels in check.

- Always include supplements to their balanced diet.

- Use paper towels, a piece of carpet, or tiles as a safe substrate.

- Regularly sanitize the enclosure to keep bacteria and parasites at bay.

- • a tab on your gecko's behavior and any anomaly you note to the vet.

Veterinarians are trained to accurately diagnose illnesses and give your gecko the best possible treatment.

# Signs of a Healthy Leopard Gecko

*20. Keep an eye out to make sure that your leopard gecko is always healthy! Source: https://www.flickr.com/photos/hellie55/24422844895*

## Clear Eyes

Healthy leopard geckos have clear eyelids without any swelling or pus.

## Responsiveness

If your gecko is running around the enclosure and actively responding to stimuli, it's a healthy sign, whereas showing a lack of responsiveness suggests an underlying problem that needs further evaluation.

## Easy Shedding

A healthy leopard gecko has lesion-free and smooth skin. Furthermore, healthy geckos shed their skin in one piece, confirming that it's well-hydrated and in great health.

## Consistent Appetite

When healthy, leopard geckos keep their appetite consistent. Furthermore, regular and well-formed bowel movements mean they have good digestive health.

## Normal Behavior

Healthy leopard geckos have normal behaviors like basking under a heat source, exploring their enclosure, and interacting with their surroundings. Unusual behavior, stress, or excessive hiding may signal health concerns.

## Normal Breathing

Observe your gecko's breathing patterns. You won't hear your gecko wheezing, gasping, or making abnormal sounds when healthy.

## How to Keep the Temperature Just Right

Healthy leopard geckos keep moving from time to time between the warm and cool areas of the enclosure to keep their temperature comfortable.

## How Often They Shed

Leopard geckos shed their skin every four to eight weeks. During the process, a healthy gecko won't have a problem shedding skin, while a leopard gecko with poor health won't be able to shed skin completely.

## Clear Nasal Passages to Breathe Easy

Nasal passages won't be clogged or discharging fluid in healthy geckos.

If you observe any signs of blockage or nasal discharge from their nostrils, contacting a vet for the necessary treatment will be the right step. Furthermore, never miss scheduled veterinary check-ups, as it can prevent many of these problems.

# Routine Care and Veterinary Visits

## Routine Care

## Enclosure

The enclosure you use must be according to the gecko's size and it's best if you use safe substrates like a carpet, paper towels, or tiles to avoid issues associated with substrates.

## Temperature and Lighting

As you already know, you must maintain a temperature gradient in the enclosure with one area around 88-90°F (31-32°C) and the other area around 75-80°F (24-27°C). Likewise, add UVB lights to let your pet make their calcium and a heat source, especially during winter.

## Hiding Spots

Include multiple hiding spots with warm and cool options to cater to the gecko's thermoregulation needs.

## Feeding

Feed a varied diet of appropriately sized live insects, dust their food with a calcium supplement (without D3) two to three times a week, and provide a multivitamin once a week.

## Hydration

The water dish you place must be shallow for easy drinking. During arid conditions, misting the enclosure with water can keep your gorgeous pet hydrated.

*21. Make sure your leopard gecko always has water so they're always hydrated. Source:*
*https://www.flickr.com/photos/elvissa/185646679*

## Cleaning

Make it a habit to keep the enclosure sanitized, as it will prevent microbial growth and create a healthy living environment.

## Handling

As leopard geckos don't like touching, always hold the gecko gently to reduce stress and wash your hands before and after contact.

---

# Veterinary Visits

Never miss any scheduled veterinary check-ups, especially if you have just bought a leopard gecko or your gecko has a history of health issues. Furthermore, don't hesitate to contact the vet if you notice an unusual sign like avoiding food, not moving much, or excessive hiding.

Remember, proactive care and regular veterinary check-ups are essential for preventing and promptly addressing health issues. Always consult with a veterinarian experienced in reptile care to treat your leopard gecko's specific needs and circumstances.

# Chapter 6: Fun Facts and Quirky Behavior

Kim believed acting differently was normal when she was out with her parents. She is usually more straight-faced and calm when they are outside. Meet Kim at home, and you'll be shocked. In the comfort of her home, Kim's otherwise straight face is wearing a smile and making funny faces for her baby brother. Her calm front is nowhere to be seen as she runs around the house noisily. Her best friend wouldn't have seen this side of her if they hadn't become friends. Kim's quirky behaviors at home, where she's comfortable, made her friends find her fun to be around.

*22. Leopard geckos are fun and quirky and always smiling! Source: https://www.rawpixel.com/image/5934510/photo-image-cco-creative-commons-wild*

Like Kim, the leopard gecko has many quirky behaviors. Understanding their behavior is important if you are going to keep them. Best friends know the most basic and weird things about each other. This makes them feel more connected to each other. This chapter will introduce you to the quirky behaviors of the leopard gecko and a ton of fun facts that will make your jaw drop.

## Unusual Behaviors of the Leopard Gecko

1. **They wag their tails a lot.** Geckos do this thing where they wave their tails back and forth like some kind of weird dance sometimes. You will catch them doing this whenever they are excited about the food you gave them or are grumpy and not in the mood to play.

2. **They lick things to identify them.** You know how you use your fingers to feel things and identify

them even without looking at them? Geckos can do that, too. But instead of using their tiny limbs, they use their tongues to taste things around them for easy identification. So don't be surprised if your gecko licks your face, it's just trying to get familiar with you.

3. **They shed their skins.** If you ever see your gecko looking a little wrinkly and dull, don't worry about it. It doesn't mean they're sick or anything. Leopard geckos, just like snakes, shed their old skin to grow even bigger and prettier. It's like getting a brand-new, shiny outfit.

4. **They tend to go glass-surfing.** Sometimes, you might catch your gecko trying to climb the walls of its tank without really going anywhere. This strange behavior, called "glass-surfing," might look like they are stuck or freaking out. But it is actually caused by stress or discomfort. To help them, you can check if everything is alright in their tank and fix the issue if you find any.

## Fun Facts That Surprise Even Adults

### Did You Know?

**Leopard geckos have eyelids!** Most geckos do not have the right body parts for the simple act of blinking. They are eyelid-less animals. They only have a glassy lens over their eyes which they clean with their tongues when it's getting dusty. But the leopard gecko is a very special species; they refuse to be thrown into the bunch. They have their own version of an eyelid, allowing them to blink and close their eyes while sleeping, just like you.

23. Leopard geckos have eyelids. Source: https://www.rawpixel.com/image/6023521/photo-image-public-domain-nature-free

**Did You Know?**

**Leopard geckos love to pull all-nighters.** They have no trouble sleeping during the day, so they can stay up at night and play around in their tank. They are usually very agile during nighttime. That's because they like the cooler temperatures and darkness. This is when they feel comfortable and relaxed enough to come out of their hiding spots to take a look at their surroundings and find insects and worms to eat.

**Did You Know?**

**Leopard geckos are one of the toughest reptiles.** Their natural habitats are rocky places where it's hot and dry, not places with rivers and lakes. Because of this, an average adult gecko doesn't need a big bowl of water to drink all the time, as other pets do. It's kind of amazing. They get most of their hydration from the food they eat. So, even though they live in a dry place, they can stay nice and hydrated.

### Did You Know?

**Leopard geckos don't have sticky toe pads like other geckos.** Most geckos are famous for their amazing climbing skills thanks to their sticky toe pads. But the leopard geckos aren't part of that community, they use their claws for grip. Their little claws are like tiny climbing picks that help them move around rocks and branches in their habitats. It's a different way of getting around, but it works just fine for them.

24. *Their little claws are like tiny climbing picks. Source:* *https://www.flickr.com/photos/kaptainkobold/2738342236*

## Unique Traits of Leopard Geckos

5. As leopard geckos grow, they become more mature, staying in one spot and observing instead of bouncing around. While young, they spent most of their time checking out new things. But once

they're grown up, they pick their favorite hiding spots and places to hang out in their tank. They have a little routine going on. This is good news for you because it makes knowing where to find them easier during feeding or cleaning time.

6. Some geckos might start acting a little weird when they reach grown-up age. They might chirp or click more, kind of like talking to themselves. This is because they're looking for a girlfriend or boyfriend.

7. Some grown-up geckos, especially the males, can get a little cranky. They might puff out their chests and want some space, saying, "No playing today, I'm busy!" They also like to mark their stuff by rubbing on things, like saying, "This is my territory; don't test me!"

8. Unlike young geckos, adult geckos don't need to eat too much. Little geckos are still developing their bodies, so they need lots of little insects to grow big and strong. But grown-up geckos are already big, so they just need a good, filling meal now and then to feel full and happy.

9. If you've been holding your gecko since it was little, it's probably used to you by now and won't mind being picked up. But every gecko is different, so some might still be shy. Don't let it bother you. Just keep hanging out with them and allow them to come to you when they are comfortable and ready. As much as you can use a leash on them, it'll be great if you don't use one. They don't like that very much. You probably wouldn't either.

From staying hydrated to climbing without sticky toes, leopard geckos are full of surprises. Don't you agree? This chapter has exposed you further to their fascinating world, exploring their quirky behaviors, unexpected facts, and unique traits that make them truly special pets. Now you'll know there's a whole lot more going on than meets the eye when you look at the leopard gecko again. Have fun with your little friend.

# Chapter 7: Engaging Activities for Children

Now that you've learned about the leopard gecko's quirky behavior and some fun facts that would surprise adults, it is time for some exciting activities for you to learn more about your leopard gecko pet. In this chapter, you will be learning how to build them a playground, and given some fun, educational games that you can play with friends and family. Trust me, you won't be bored here. Are you ready for the wonders of engaging with these cute lizards? First, let's talk a little about how you can safely handle your gecko.

*25. There are many fun activities you can do with your new best friend!*
*Source:*
*https://www.flickr.com/photos/21053413@N07/7477062184/*

## Safe Handling Techniques

Handling a leopard gecko requires care and attention to ensure the gecko's well-being and safety. It's great that you want to carry your gecko everywhere with you, but you must do so with utmost care and gentleness to guarantee both your and the gecko's safety. Here are some easy tips to help you with that:

- Keep a bowl of water and some soap on standby always, so you can wash your hands before and after you pick up your gecko. Make this a tradition so that it becomes a habit, like washing your hands before eating.

- The gecko is quite fragile, so you don't want to squeeze them too tight when you pick them up. It could scare you and try to wriggle away from you. So, get used to holding the gecko with your hands, gently cupping its whole body.

- Don't raise your voice at your gecko. Speak to it softly and calmly wait for it to find its way toward you.

- If you have younger siblings or friends who want to hold the gecko, don't leave them to handle the gecko themselves, hand around and watch them closely. Leopard geckos are small and fragile, so you don't want anyone to drop them.

- Know when to stop touching them. If your gecko seems stressed or tries to escape, put them back in their enclosure immediately. They probably just want some space or some time to themselves. Respect their wish, and give them some privacy.

Some geckos are cuddlier than others. So be patient and let your gecko get used to you at its own pace. If you want to learn even more about how to hold your gecko safely, many great books and websites about leopard geckos can help.

# DIY Enrichment Ideas

Remember Tanner? Well, he found some things at home, and when he went to the store with his mom, he used to add some really cool designs to his gecko's tank. Things like a mini ladder, which he created, some plastic plants etc. These things are called DIY enrichment. Think of it like creating a personal playground for your leopard gecko to keep its mind active. Like you, leopard geckos love to explore and have fun, and you can give them that by getting some great stuff for their tank. Here are some DIY enrichment ideas to keep your gecko entertained:

- **Turn their home into a mini jungle away from forests.** Use fake plants (the safe kind for pets, of course) or even real ones that are okay for geckos. Add some rocks and hiding spots for them to climb and explore.

- **Build a climbing wall for them.** You can use plastic pipes (make sure they aren't too sharp) or cork bark to make a climbing wall for your gecko.

- **Instead of just putting their food in a dish, try hiding it around their tank.** This makes them work a little for their dinner, like playing a fun hunting game.

- **Tickle their feet with stones.** Put some rough stones or special reptile sand in their tank. It will feel interesting under their little toes and keep them exploring.

# Educational Games about Leopard Geckos

Learning about leopard geckos through educational games can be a lot of fun. These selected games will help you think creatively, solve problems, and become a leopard gecko expert.

## Mystery Gecko Cafe

Materials: Construction paper, crayons, markers, scissors, and glue.

**Instructions:**

1.  Find pictures of different parts of the leopard gecko. If you can't find any, then draw some. You can also add some drawings of insects like crickets, grasshoppers, and locusts, which the gecko usually feeds on.

2.  Cut out the pictures piece by piece and glue them onto separate pieces of construction paper.

3.  Flip the cards over and take turns picking two. You win that round if you get a matching pair (eye with eye, cricket with cricket).

This game helps you learn and identify different parts of a leopard gecko's body and diet.

# Create Your Dream Terrarium

*26. You can create and decorate your terrarium. Source: https://commons.wikimedia.org/wiki/File:Eublepharis_maculariu s_in_Tropicarium-Oceanarium_Budapest_01.JPG*

## Materials:

- Cardboard box

- Crayons

- Markers

- Construction paper

- Scissors

- Glue

- Paper towel rolls

## Instructions:

1. Get a clean and empty cardboard. This would be at the bottom of your terrarium.

2. Use the construction paper to create different areas in the box that would serve as your gecko's hiding or basking spots.

3. Cut paper towel rolls in half to make tunnels and use popsicle sticks to create climbing structures.

4. Let your imagination run wild. This activity helps you understand the elements needed in a proper leopard gecko habitat.

## The Great Gecko Guessing Game

**Materials:** None needed (observe your pet gecko or pictures online).

**Instructions:**

1. Players (you and your friends or family members) take turns observing a leopard gecko, either live or online, for a few minutes.

2. Each writes down questions about the gecko, such as "What color are its spots?"

3. Players take turns asking each other the questions and see who can guess the answers correctly. This activity forces you to closely observe the gecko to learn about their behavior.

## Leopard Gecko Life Cycle Scrapbook

**Materials:**

- Paper
- Pencils

- Crayons

- Markers

**Instructions:**

1.  Find out the stages of a leopard gecko's life cycle - egg, hatchling, juvenile, and adult.

2.  Fold a piece of paper into squares to create panels for your comic strip.

3.  On each side, draw a picture depicting a stage in the gecko's life cycle and write a short caption describing what's happening.

To make this even more fun, you can create a file to record all the amazing things you've learned about leopard geckos. You can call this file the "Gecko fact file". All these games are designed to teach you about leopard geckos and improve your creativity, critical thinking, and sense of responsibility.

Taking care of a leopard gecko teaches you to be kind to animals and responsible for other living things. It gives you a glimpse of how cool nature is. You have learned how to gently hold geckos, build them a fun play area in their tank, and play games to become a gecko expert. Sooner or later, you'll be the one other children come to ask questions about the leopard gecko. Keep being awesome.

# Chapter 8: Frequently Asked Questions

Welcome to the final chapter of your leopard gecko adventure with this book. You're the true definition of a champion. Now, let's take a look at some of the frequently asked questions about the leopard gecko. Buckle up because from these common concerns, you will learn even more about your pet and understand their behavior much better. Keep reading to continue building your portfolio as a leopard gecko expert.

## Addressing Common Concerns

### Are leopard geckos good pets?

Leopard geckos have a gentle disposition and are generally considered easier to care for than other reptiles. Their diet and nutrition requirements are not a stretch at all. Give them insects, and they are good to go. They don't need a massive tank, so you don't need to worry about them taking up too much space in your room. They are very friendly and confident creatures. You should get yourself one.

## How big a tank does my leopard gecko need?

An adult leopard gecko needs a 20-gallon enclosure long tank. The length of the tank allows them ample room to move around without having to hit the objects in their tanks too often. Leopard geckos mostly stay on the ground, so don't bother getting a tall tank. They prefer to explore the ground and move along the substrate rather than climbing vertically. You can keep a baby leopard gecko in something much smaller. They are scared of big open spaces.

## What kind of food do leopard geckos eat?

Leopard geckos eat crickets, mealworms, cockroaches, locusts, cutworms etc. You can offer them some wax worms sometimes as snacks or treats. Those are best served once or twice. You don't want your gecko to become addicted to these worms because they have high fat. Make sure the insects you give them are not bigger than the space between your gecko's eyes.

## Why is my gecko not eating?

Your gecko's appetite can change from time to time, especially if they have been under stress. This usually happens when they are first introduced to a new environment. But don't worry. The hunger strike won't last long. It's only until they become familiar with their surroundings. But if your gecko still doesn't eat after a long time, then it is time to visit a vet. They could be suffering from a bacterial infection or a parasite.

## Why does my gecko shed its skin?

Leopard geckos shedding their skin is kind of like how you change your clothes. But instead of using their hands, they use their teeth to peel off the old skin. This allows for the growth of fresh and healthy skin. They need the shed to come off to stay healthy.

## Do leopard geckos need special lights?

Leopard geckos need a warm basking spot to keep their body temperature just right. They are cold-blooded animals. The best way to create this spot for them is by getting a heat lamp with a thermostat, which will help create a cool to warm temperature from one side to another inside their tank.

## Q: How often do I need to clean my gecko's tank?

Spot clean waste daily and do a full tank clean every few months. This includes removing all the substrate and decorations, cleaning the tank with a reptile-safe cleaner, and replacing the substrate with fresh stuff.

# Troubleshooting Tips for New Leopard Gecko Owners

**My gecko fell:** Depending on the distance and the impact of the fall, you can just pick them back up. They might sustain an injury or, worse break a limb. When this happens, don't hesitate to take them to a vet. There might be other damages caused by the fall.

**My gecko's tail looks strange:** Leopard geckos store fat in their tails, so changes in tail appearance could indicate health issues. Tail loss (autotomy) is common in geckos under stress or if their tail is grabbed. Ensure your gecko's habitat is stress-free, and avoid handling them roughly.

**My gecko's shed got stuck:** After your leopard gecko sheds its skin, check for any leftover pieces that might be stuck. While they usually shed all at once, sometimes they get a little stuck, especially on their toes, tail, or head. If the stuck shed isn't removed, it can actually cut off circulation to their toes and cause them to fall off. Help them remove the stuck shed.

**My leopard gecko screams when I come near it:** Don't worry, this is pretty common with young leopard geckos. Just like human babies cry, young geckos "scream" to scare off anything they think might be a threat. It's their natural way of saying "back off!" This happens because:

10. Young geckos are tiny and don't know any better. They see a big giant (you) coming near and get scared.

11. They are trying to scare you away, so they puff up their body and make a loud squeaking sound. It might surprise you, but it probably works on some predators.

The good news is that your gecko should stop screaming as they get older and more used to you. Just be patient and gentle when you're around them.

My leopard gecko doesn't trust me: Leopard geckos can be friendly and curious animals, but they need time to feel comfortable with you. If you want to build trust with your gecko so you can eventually hold them, follow these steps:

1. **Let them get used to you.** Sit near their tank and talk softly for the first week or so. The more you do this, the more they get accustomed to your presence and voice. Once they start recognizing your voice, you can also introduce them to your unique scent. Try wearing a particular scent every time you visit it or place something with your scent inside their tank.

2. **Introduce them to your hand.** You can simply put your hand inside their tank so they can play it. If your gecko approaches, let them explore your hand for as long as they want. Don't try to pick them up yet. Once they seem comfortable with your hand, offer a yummy insect. This way, they know that whenever you come around the tank, they are likely going to be fed.

3. **Gradually start handling them.** After a while, try gently scooping them up from under their belly with your hand. Support their entire body and keep the handling session short and calm. Once they're comfortable being held, let them walk around on your hand or lap.

4. **Take your time.** Just like building trust with people takes time, so it is too with geckos. They won't come around if you keep forcing them to interact. Respect their boundaries and treat them well. If your gecko seems stressed or wants to be left alone, put them back in their tank and give them some space to breathe.

## Additional Resources for Further Learning

Here are some resources to keep you learning all about leopard geckos, with a mix of books, websites, and videos to give you all the information you need:

### Books

1. The Leopard Gecko Manual by Philippe de Vosjoli.

2. Leopard Geckos for Dummies by Kelly Hatfield.

3. Leopard Geckos by Pete Hawkins.

4. The Complete Care of Leopard Geckos by Martina Hajkova.

5. Leopard Geckos as Pets by Richard Francaviglia.

## Websites

1. Leopard Gecko Care Sheet (https://reptifiles.com/leopard-gecko-care/)

2. Reptile Guide | Leopard Gecko New Owner's Guide (https://reptile.guide/leopard-gecko-care/)

3. Fluker Farms | Leopard Gecko Care Sheet (https://flukerfarms.com/reptile-u/care-sheets/leopard-gecko-care-sheet)

4. Leopard Gecko | Reptile Magazine (https://reptilesmagazine.com/listings/lizards-care-sheets/leopard-gecko/)

## YouTube Videos

1. Leopard Gecko Care Guide for Beginners [Leopard Gecko Tank Setup & Info] by Snake Discovery. (https://www.youtube.com/watch?v=4g_vMdx25LM)

2. How To Tame A Leopard Gecko [Ultimate Guide] by Victoria Rachael. (https://www.youtube.com/watch?v=7_9QBFHNtUg)

3. Leopard Gecko BREEDING Guide for Beginners [Everything You Need To Know!] by Leopard

Gecko Tube
(https://m.youtube.com/watch?v=iVbPi_NAobg)

# Conclusion

Leopard geckos are some of the easiest creatures to understand. Their behavior is straightforward and can be cared for without much hassle. They are also adorable, to boot. The information in this book is easy to understand but quite extensive. The summary below is to help you process it better.

You started with a brief overview of leopard geckos, their alternate name, general habitat, feeding habits, and more. They are popular as pets among children and adults alike, but they are especially great for the former because they make excellent starter pets.

The second chapter focused on their physical characteristics, from their long tail and tiny indentations to their dorsal spots and color variety. At this point, their wild habitat was explored in great detail (arid regions, rocky terrain, etc.).

Then, you learned how to make the perfect terrarium for your favorite pets. The tank should be at least 10 gallons in size, and the substrate should be a mixture of soil, sand, and clay. Proper temperature should be maintained, and necessary, appropriate accessories should be provided.

Their feeding habits followed. They prefer meat, but you should also provide vegetables to maintain their health. If they face any health problems, don't hesitate to take them to the vet. Typically, healthy geckos have bright eyes and a thick tail.

In the next chapter, you discovered a few fun facts about your leopard geckos that would impress even adults. The final pages described a long list of activities you can do to make your time with your pet ten times more interesting!

**Key Takeaways**

- Leopard geckos have eyelids unlike most other lizards.

- They can live up to 20 years with proper care.

- They need space to move around in the terrarium.

- They eat both insects and fresh vegetables.

- They can produce a variety of sounds but prefer to stay quiet.

# References

Are Reptiles a Good Pet for Kids? (2018). Zilla.
https://www.zillarules.com/articles/are-reptiles-a-good-pet-for-kids

Barrington, K. (2022, May 10). The 5 Best Terrariums, Habitats & Tank
Setups for Leopard Geckos. We're All about Pets.
https://wereallaboutpets.com/best-terrarium-habitat-tank-setup-for-
leopard-geckos

David, J. (2021, January 15). What Do Leopard Geckos Eat? Best Food
List, Diet & Feeding. Everything Reptiles.
https://www.everythingreptiles.com/what-do-leopard-geckos-eat/

Healey, M. (2024). Leopard Gecko Handling & Body Language Guide.
ReptiFiles®, LLC. https://reptifiles.com/leopard-gecko-care/leopard-
gecko-handling-body-language/

How To Setup a Leopard Gecko Terrarium? (2019, January 17). Care
Guides for Pet Lizards. https://www.lizards101.com/how-to-setup-a-
leopard-gecko-terrarium/

Information | 50 |. (n.d.). Leopard Geckos & Their Behavior.
LeopardGeckoLand.com. https://leopardgeckoland.com/about-leopard-
geckos-their-behavior/

Kruzer, A. (2022, November 29). What Colors Do Leopard Geckos Come
In? The Spruce Pets. https://www.thesprucepets.com/leopard-gecko-
morphs-1239170

Milligan, P. (2021, October 22). Species Profile - Leopard Gecko,
Eublepharis macularius. Evolution Reptiles.

https://www.evolutionreptiles.co.uk/blog/species-profile-leopard-gecko-eublepharis-macularius/

Petrov, A. (2023, August 21). Leopard Gecko Behavior 101: What Every Owner Needs to Know. ReptileBreeds.com. https://reptilebreeds.com/leopard-gecko-behavior/

Preheim, A. (2023, July 29). How Much and How Often Do You Feed Leopard Geckos? Www.morereptiles.com. https://www.morereptiles.com/how-often-do-you-feed-leopard-gecko

Rasmussen, M. H. (2022). Gecko Feet Are Coated in an Ultra-Thin Layer of Lipids That Help Them Stay Sticky. NIST. https://www.nist.gov/news-events/news/2022/07/gecko-feet-are-coated-ultra-thin-layer-lipids-help-them-stay-sticky

Repmasters Team. (2023, April 10). Leopard Gecko Personality Type: A Jumpstart Guide - Reptile Masters. Reptile Masters. https://reptilemasters.com/leopard-gecko-personality-type/

Rodriguez, M. (2023, February 11). Building A Leopard Gecko Terrarium: The Ultimate Guide. Leopard Gecko Planet. https://leopardgeckoplanet.com/building-a-leopard-gecko-terrarium/

Samurovic, K. (2018, April 1). Leopard Gecko Habitat: A Guide to the Ideal Tank Setup. Terrarium Quest. https://www.terrariumquest.com/leopard-gecko/habitat/

Stacey. (2021, March 31). Leopard Gecko Morphs [the Ultimate Guide] - Reptile.Guide. Reptile.guide. https://reptile.guide/leopard-gecko-morphs/

Sutton, C. (2023, January 24). 10 Vet Reviewed Common Diseases in Leopard Geckos (& Care Tips). Pet Keen. https://petkeen.com/common-diseases-in-leopard-geckos/

Tony. (2014, April 7). Basic Leopard Gecko Tank Setup - Leopard Gecko Care. Leopard Gecko Care. https://leopardgeckocare.net/leopard-gecko-terrarium-vivarium-setup/

Wright, S. (2023, May 1). 20 Fun Facts About Leopard Geckos - Gecko Advice. Geckoadvice.com. https://geckoadvice.com/leopard-gecko-facts/

Hiller, E. (2019, August 15). 5 Leopard Gecko Handling Tips & 1 Thing to Never Do! Leopard Gecko Habitat.

https://leopardgeckohabitat.com/how-to-handle-and-tame-a-leopard-gecko/

Lee, R. (2020, September 21). The Pet Enthusiast. TPE. https://thepetenthusiast.com/leopard-gecko-enrichment/

Lizard 101. (2019, January 13). Fun Things To Do With a Leopard Gecko. Care Guides for Pet Lizards. https://www.lizards101.com/fun-things-to-do-with-a-leopard-gecko/

Oddblog. (2022). 12 Leopard Gecko Enrichment Ideas. Https://Oddlycutepets.com/. https://oddlycutepets.com/leopard-gecko-enrichment/

Petrov, A. (2023, September 25). Leopard Gecko Handling 101: Creating a Positive Experience. ReptileBreeds.com. https://reptilebreeds.com/leopard-gecko-handling/

Ryan, B. (2021, March 12). Providing Enrichment for your Gecko. Gecko Time. https://geckotime.com/providing-enrichment-for-your-gecko/

Aliza. (2014, March 12). What's Going On With My New Leopard Gecko? Gecko Time. https://geckotime.com/whats-going-on-with-my-new-leopard-gecko/

Miller, H. (2022). Common Mistakes New Leopard Gecko Owners Make. Leopard Gecko Habitat. https://leopardgeckohabitat.com/mistakes-new-leopard-gecko-owners-make/

Morethanagecko. (2019, May 9). Tips for new leopard gecko owners. More than Gecko. https://morethanagecko.wordpress.com/2019/05/09/tips-for-new-or-future-leopard-gecko-owners/

Stacey. (2020, June 6). Leopard Gecko Care Sheet: Your One Stop Know It All Guide (Must Read!). Reptile Guide. https://reptile.guide/leopard-gecko-care/

Super Pets. (2020, January 19). A Helpful Leopard Gecko Care Guide For New Owners. Super Crazy Pets. https://supercrazypets.com/leopard-gecko-care-guide/

Printed in Great Britain
by Amazon

63080957R00047